History Of Europe For Kids

A History Series

Children Explore Histories Of The World Edition

SPEEDY
PUBLISHING

Speedy Publishing LLC
40 E. Main St. #1156
Newark, DE 19711
www.speedypublishing.com

The history of Europe covers the peoples inhabiting the European continent from after prehistoric times to the present.

In the beginning, there was no Europe—all that existed was an unpopulated peninsula attached to the western edge of the world's largest landmass (Asia).

It was in Greece and Rome that the continent's two great ancient societies arose.

Throughout history, Europe has been the scene of many great and destructive wars that have ravaged both rural and urban areas.

By the 4th century AD both empires were in terminal decline. Greece had been swallowed by Macedonia under Alexander the Great, then by Rome itself in AD 146.

From 768 Charlemagne, King of the Franks, brought together much of Western Europe under his rule into what would later be known as the 'Holy Roman Empire'.

The Renaissance fomented mainly artistic expression and ideas.

The Age of Reason in the 18th century when science and human logic for the first time took supremacy over religious belief.

The French Revolution in 1789 was about the populace's attempt to wrest political power from the monarchy.

Having vanquished Napoleon, Britain became a major world player itself. With the invention of the steam engine, railways and factories, it unleashed the Industrial Revolution.

Crippled by a huge bill for reparations imposed at the war's end in 1918, Austria's humbled ally, Germany, proved susceptible to politician Adolf Hitler's nationalist rhetoric during the 1930s.

During the final liberation of Europe in 1945, Allied troops from Britain, France, the USA and the USSR uncovered the full extent of the genocide that had occurred in Hitler's concentration camps for Jews, Roma (Gypsies), the disabled, homosexuals, communists and other 'degenerates'.

Differences in ideology between the Western powers and the communist USSR soon led to a stand-off.

The 'Cold War' lasted until 1989 when the Berlin Wall fell.

Germany was unified in 1990.

In 1991, the USSR was dissolved.

Czechoslovakia, Hungary, Poland, Romania, Bulgaria and Albania all grasped multiparty democracy.

ФІНАНСОВУ БАЗУ
БУДОВИ СОЦІЯЛІЗМУ
у виконанні плану
ПЕРЕХІДНИЙ ПРАПОР

After World War II, Europe became divided into two ideological blocs (Eastern Europe, dominated by the USSR, and Western Europe, dominated by the United States) and became engaged in the cold war.

The European History is very interesting, research and learn more!